The Fishin_

Wilf and Dan went to catch fish.

Wilf had his fishing rod and a can with grubs in it. Dan was splashing. "Stop it! The elf dust will get wet," said Wilf.

Wilf began to nod off. A bag of elf

dust fell from his pocket. Dan

snatched the elf dust. "I wish I was

as big as that frog!" Dan was thinking.

Flash! Whizz! Dan felt himself

shrinking. "I am shrinking!" said Dan

to himself. All of a sudden, Dan was

sitting next to the frog in the pond.

Dan and the frog jumped into the pond. "Let's go swimming with the fish," said Dan. Dan and the frog swam in the glinting pond.

Just then, Dan felt a thing grabbing his jacket. It snatched him up. Dan began kicking and splashing. Dan was hanging from the end of a fishing rod.

"Let me go!" begged Dan. Flash! Dan was a big kid again. "Elf dust is not for kids," said Wilf. "But swimming with a frog was such fun," said Dan, grinning.

Reading practice and lotto game

Use this page as a two-syllable reading exercise.
You can also photocopy this page and use it to play as a lotto game.
Enlarge and photocopy the set of cards twice on different
coloured card. Cut up one set to make the cards. Cut the other
page in half to make two bases.

check/ing checking	dropp/ing dropping	slamm/ing slamming
sniff/ing sniffing	scrapp/ing scrapping	thrill/ing thrilling

shrink/ing shrinking	spitt/ing spitting	mend/ing mending
glint/ing glinting	swimm/ing swimming	thump/ing thumping